Group Study and Personal Reflection Guide
for:
When the Northern Lights Went Dark

My Journey through Loss and Grief to Healing and Hope

Rev. Dr. Brian L. Erickson
brianerickson50@gmail.com

Blog: *Meandering Spirituality*
www.pastorbrianerickson.blogspot.com

*Master of Divinity and
Doctor of Ministry*
**Luther Theological Seminary,
Saint Paul, MN**

This book is dedicated to my grandson, Dylan Edrei Melton-Erickson. (See back cover) He proves that the journey through grief, although long and hard, is worth the trip. This study guide is written in the hope that it will help others make that journey.

All page numbers reference the original book.

Contents

Part I   The Search for One's Self

Part II   Seasons of Life and Love

Part III   The Long Journey Home

Chapter 9

Chapter 10

Chapter 11

Chapter 12

Preface

This **Group Study and Personal Reflection Guide** is written to accompany my book on loss and grief, **When the Northern Lights Went Dark: My Journey through Loss and Grief to Healing and Hope.**

That book is not a book "about" grief, but rather a book "of" grief. I tell the story of losing both of my parents to death in high school and then my wife, Pauline, to death when we were both 32. This narrative includes journal entries written by Pauline as she was facing death, and by me the year after she died as I struggled with grief.

Throughout the book I share insights about the process of grieving and the search for new meaning in life. The purpose of this study guide is to highlight those insights and offer observations and questions--as one moves through the book alone, or as a group-- for further reflection and discussion. It also offers an opportunity to do your own journaling as you reflect on your own experiences of loss and grief as you continue to search for healing and hope.

As I wrote in the Introduction to my book: "In what follows I share the losses that have shaped me, and what I have learned from them, not so that you can get to know me, but so that you can get to know yourself. I believe that the most particular is also the most universal, and that my story will lead you deeper into your own story as you try to understand who you are and why you are the way you are. As you do that, I am pretty sure that you will love yourself even more." (11-12)

Introduction (10)

"My life has been shaped by loss." (10) Grief is our response to loss, and the only path to healing and hope is through the courage to grieve. And it takes a lot of courage to actually grieve.

A common conception you hear often is that "time heals." That is not really true. It is grieving that heals, which does not automatically happen with time. In fact, it is possible to get "stuck" in grief, and to go long periods without making much progress.

This book deals primarily with my losses to death, along with a few other types of loss. What are the primary losses you have experienced in your life, which may come from death, abuse, trauma, a sense of failure, or a host of other areas of life?

Prologue: Graves (13)

I suggest in the Prologue that graves, while tempting to avoid, can actually become places of healing, reconciliation, forgiveness, revelation and renewed hope. (14) What has been your experience with graves? Do you stay away from them? Are there any graves you go to visit regularly? What feelings do those visits conjure up for you?

Chapter 1: Dad (18)

One of the most common emotions regarding our losses is **guilt.** (27, 35) This guilt occurs when we feel that we handled something—or didn't handle something--in a way we later regret.

One of the main sources of guilt is the **denial** which occurs because we are afraid of loss and find all kinds of ways to pretend it is not happening. I tried to deny that my father was dying, which led to my avoiding being with him, which eventually led to guilt.

Are there important areas of your life where you are in denial? Have you handled experiences in a way that has led you to feel guilty?

Over and over again through my grieving experiences I discovered that the presence of others (and their tears) was an essential step toward my healing. One example of this is all of the Bible camp counselors wo came to my dad's funeral (33).

Have you experienced this kind of loving presence in your life? Do you find that you try to be present for others when they are suffering, or do you find this difficult to do? If so, what holds you back?

14

Chapter 2: Mom (37)

In what ways have you experienced "layering," (41) where "questions and insights pile up over the years?" Regarding losses you have experienced, what are the questions you still wonder about? If you have lost a loved one to death, are there any questions you would like to ask that person now? If you have questions, do you have any idea how that loved one would answer you?

Because it is "very difficult to go back and correctly unpeel the layering," I suggest that "we learn how to live in grace, and not torment ourselves because we did not ask certain questions when we had the chance." (41) To what extent are you able to treat yourself graciously?

18

Have there been times when you have avoided grieving by "keeping busy" and adhering to a routine? (49) In what ways was this helpful, and in what ways has it not been helpful?

Throughout the book I suggest that one of the main avenues of healing grief is the opportunity to talk about our pain and loss, over and over again. However, often those around us fear that bringing up our loss will increase our pain. (50) What has been your experience with this dynamic, either as one who has grieved or as one who is trying to support one who is grieving?

20

One of the primary emotions I began to feel toward Mom was anger. (52-53, 69) This anger may have been somewhat irrational and unfair, but it was a powerful feeling none the less. Have you had this experience? If so, where have you directed your anger? Did you find that to be helpful or not?

One of the themes of this book is the importance of having an open conversation with loved ones who are dying, including asking for forgiveness if we feel badly about anything and expressing our love to the person who is dying. I did not have this experience with my dad, but I did with my mom. (55)

Have you had any experiences talking with a loved one shortly before they died? What was that experience like for you? Have you lost anyone without the opportunity to talk with them shortly before they died? How are you dealing with that now? Can you think of anything you might do to bring further healing?

22

Over the years I became convinced my mother died of a "broken heart." (47, 67) Have you witnessed someone dying in that way? Has your heart ever been broken in a way that you wondered if you could ever find lasting healing?

Chapter 3: Thrust from the Womb (60)

Another kind of loss I began to experience after Mom's and Dad's deaths was conflict with my older brother over finances and Mom's will. (66-67) We all hope that in times of loss and grief our families will come together in a loving and supportive way. However, sometimes loss and grief can actually lead to misunderstanding and separation. Have you experienced that in your life, or seen it happen to someone you know?

24

"One of the most difficult things about life is that loss and tragedy often are not self-contained. One experience of suffering sometimes leads to, if not causes, another." (67)

Have you ever had this experience in life? If so, how did you handle it? Is such a chain-reaction inevitable, or are there things we can do to try to break the chain?

Chapter 4: Rebirth (75)

On p. 92, speaking of the death of my friend, Pat, I refer to two types of grief. I also refer to these two types of grief regarding the death of my childhood friend, Billy. (128-129)

One type of grief, with which we are most familiar, is losing something that is precious to us. The second is the loss of something that we wanted, but never experienced. This could be a relationship that was not the way we hoped it would be--as when my older brother, Neil, disowned me for a period of seven years--(93-94), someone dying young---as in the case of Pat--or not experiencing something we wanted to experience, such as marriage, success at work, giving birth, having a grandchild, etc.

Have you ever experienced this second form of grief?

Can you also think of times that you may have made peace with either type of grief? If so, what helped you to be able do that?

Chapter 5: Spring (100)

While in clinical training in Boston, I had a powerful experience of healing of the guilt I felt towards Dad, beginning with dreams I had about him. (117-118) Have you ever had dreams that you experienced as trying to heal you in some way?

30

Have you ever had the experience of talking about something with which you are struggling--with a friend, therapist, group, etc.--where all of a sudden you experienced a revelation that brought healing?

One could perhaps think of this kind of cathartic experience as a kind of liturgical (theological) or therapeutic (psychological) "confession." Do you believe such a confession can make a dramatic change in how someone views a painful experience?

32

Do you think it is possible that we often deny ourselves healing because we are so afraid of confession and honest conversation about our struggles in life?

Chapter 6: Summer (125)

Throughout this book I struggle with the relationship of God to human suffering. In my early years I was taught (and believed) that everything that happens is God's will. On pp. 134-135 I describe a class I took which helped me rethink this theology. I began to believe that God does not **cause** our suffering, but is **with us** in our suffering. What is your view of the relationship of God to suffering?

34

My earlier theology caused me to be angry at God for taking the lives of my mom and dad. Have you felt that kind of anger at God? Have you experienced the presence of God through believing that God is with you in your suffering?

36

Pauline writes about her struggle with "self-pity." (141) We tend to think of this as an unhealthy emotion. Are there ways in which it can be a helpful step towards becoming what Pauline terms a "total person?"

On p. 144 I write that "the reality of death intensifies life." Have you experienced this in your life? How do you understand the relationship of the reality of death for each of us to the ways in which we try to live out our lives with meaning and purpose.?

Chapter 7: Autumn (146)

Pauline writes about her desire to "touch more people's lives" and be a "servant." (152) How do you understand this **calling** in your life? Would you think about it differently if you believed that death in the near future was a real possibility for you?

40

As Pauline reflects on her life, she, at the age of 31, feels she has already been to the spiritual "mountaintop." (154) She doesn't want to die, but she can accept death if it comes.

As you contemplate your own spiritual journey, do you feel that way? If not, how would you change your life? How would you change your focus and how you spend your time? In the words of the late poet, Mary Oliver: "Tell me, what is it you plan to do with your one wild and precious life?"

What is your reaction to and understanding of Pauline's journal entry that describes the end of Holy Week as a "microcosm of life?" (156-157)

How does "love as letting go" relate to her understanding of Easter Sunday? (157)

Facing death, Pauline searches for a "deeper spirituality" that will help her to become "more in tune with God." (159-161) In your own spiritual journey, where are you when it comes to focusing on your own "inner life and peace?"

44

Pauline struggles with what we call "faith healing," where miraculous healing comes through another person. (164) If you were dying, and a "faith healer" wanted to come and pray over you, what would you do?

Chapter 8: Winter (166)

Are there ways in which you repress and deny the possibility of your own death or those around you? (168) In what ways is this helpful, and in what ways is it not.

46

On pp. 184-185 I give Pauline permission to die.

Have you ever had the experience of being with someone who kept holding on to life until a certain event occurred? Do you ever think we prolong the pain of our loved ones because we don't give them permission to die?

What are your thoughts and feelings about Pauline's last journal entry, written on May 22, less than two months before she dies? (185-186)

Chapter 9: Blue Flowers, Blue Casket (189)

Early in my grief, I talk about "belongings:" Pauline's "effects" as I leave the hospital, (189) seeing her things in our Palo Alto apartment, seeing her and our things in our home in Hemet. (189-191) What is it about "belongings" that are so powerful for us? What do they trigger within us?

50

Many cultures to this day, at times of death, "wail" and "lament." Why are we so uncomfortable with both in our culture? Is this healthy or not? (192)

I also talk about "sentimental theology," wherein people share "pious phrases" that actually irritate more than they help. (192) This raises several issues when it comes to comforting and supporting those who are grieving:

What are the best things to say and not to say when someone is grieving?

52

When someone is newly grieving, is it wise to share our psychological and theological assumptions ("she's better off now," "she is over her suffering," "he's in heaven now," "he is reunited with those he loved," "God needed another angel.") How can this be dangerous and not helpful?

My own experience in grief and in working with those who are grieving is that when someone has just experienced a severe loss, they are not at the point where they are interested in a theological discussion. I believe one of the best things we can do right after a loss is to share how much we appreciated the person who has died, and what that person means to us. That is enough: often, more than enough.

What are your thoughts about this?

54

What has been your experience with graveside funeral customs? (196-197) What is helpful about them? What is not? Are there things you would change, in terms of what is said and what is done?

Chapter 10: Empty Home, Empty World (198)

Have you ever experienced the "day after" a significant loss when all of a sudden you find yourself alone? (199) What was that like for you?

Have you ever had an emotional experience wherein you feel lonely as the world just seems to keep going its merry way, oblivious to what you are feeling? (199) If so, what was that like at work, school, or even with your friends and family?

I write on p. 200 that "each retelling of stories, each sharing of memories, each tear shed, brings a touch of healing that chips away at the mountain of grief." Have you experienced this to be true? If it is, how does that inform the way we care for those who are grieving, and what we need to try to do when we are the ones grieving?

58

I wrote earlier of my belief that my mother died, in part, from a "broken heart." On pp. 200 and 206 I relate how I wished in a way that death would come to me. Have you ever lost someone so dear to you that you wondered whether your own life was still worth living? Have you ever had another kind of loss that made you wonder if you still want to live, or if you can handle the pain?

60

On pp. 201-202 I relate an experience in which Pauline did (or seemed to) appear to me to help heal me. Have you ever had an experience like that? If so, what was the message you received from it?

In my grieving I write about the difficulty of the evenings and nights, including driving home to a "dark home." (203) Have you ever had that experience? If so, what was it like for you?

62

On p. 204 I relate an experience wherein my own deep sense of loss helped me understand better my mother's "broken heart." Have you ever had an experience where you had to go through a painful event yourself before you could finally understand what someone else was going through?

On p. 207 I write that "we seem to have an innate need for (our loved one's) suffering and death to somehow make a difference," and I share three examples. My own experience was that of wanting to share Pauline's journal entries about death and dying and to promote transplant organ donations.

Can you understand why this might be important to a person? Do you think it helps the healing process or not?

64

Going deeper: When we try to comfort those grieving (including trying to comfort ourselves when we are grieving) we often spend time focusing on how the loved one died, if anything different should have been done, how something good might come out of their death, how we might get retribution if we think someone contributed to their death, etc. However, if grief is the loss of the presence of the one we love so dearly, how important, really, are any of these other things? Is it possible they might actually serve as a kind of wall that keeps us from facing our deep loss head on and going "straight through it"-- as I write in the book-- rather than around, under, or over it?

66

On p. 209 I write about the positive and negative things I did (or did not do) in terms of confronting my own grief, including support groups and professional counseling which I did not take advantage of.

What are your thoughts and experience with these two avenues of healing?

Two things I did do was to call on my friend, Chuck, on a regular basis and to keep journaling, as Pauline did. Do you have that kind of friend when and if you experience a significant loss? Have you ever journaled as a path toward understanding and healing?

68

On pp. 210-211 I share how I never want to forget and have completely healed the holes in my heart that I carry for those whom I love who have died. I go on to talk about how I just wanted the gaping wound to be scarred over, but not completely healed. Does this make any sense to you? Have you ever had this kind of experience or feeling?

On pp. 212-213 I write about how some family and friends were more supportive than I thought they would be, and that I was somewhat surprised (and disappointed) by how some others could not stand by Pauline and me. Have you ever had that experience? If so, why do you think it is so difficult for some people to be supportive in the way we hope they will be?

Chapter 11: A Heart in a Tomb (214)

On pp. 214-216 I describe an experience that I label "violation," wherein you share something intimate and precious to you, and then feel it is being rejected. Have you ever had that experience? If so, what was it like for you?

I point out that such violating experiences can become a "stumbling block" to "healing and wholeness," writing further: "If healing comes by walking through grief with others, then anything that causes us to close in on ourselves and quit sharing our feelings hinders the healing process." (216)

When we are in grief, what does this tell us about what we need to do?

If we are trying to support someone who is grieving, what can we do to help that person feel safe and open about sharing what is really going on for them?

74

On p. 217 I write about the experience of watching someone suffer and even approach death, and feeling so "helpless" in terms of being able to protect the one we love from pain, suffering or death. Have you had that experience? If so, what was it (is it) like for you?

Chapter 12: Good Friday: The Valley of Death (220)

Carolos Santana sang a song, written by Leon Patilla, that goes:

> Try a little harder now
>
> No one ever said it would be easy
> Doin' whatever you do
> You just might have to suffer
> But keep on movin' right through
> You've got to
>
> Try a little harder now
> Try a little harder now.

On p. 221 I state that one way I tried to deal with my grief was through "positive thinking" and "trying a little harder." How much does this help? Are there ways in which it might actually impede healing?

78

On pp. 224-225 I reflect on the meaning that comes with being in solidarity with fellow travelers in the journey of grief. Have you experienced the power of such community and solidarity when you have grieved? Have you found meaning in trying to "stand by" others in their times of suffering?

Chapter 13: Goodbye Yellow Brick Road (226)

As I began to find some healing, one of the thoughts that kept going through my mind, as written on p. 226, was this: "If I am still alive, then God must have a purpose for me, and I need to figure out now what that purpose is."

Does that statement ring true to you in any way? Can you think of times in your life (including right now) when you wonder what your purpose in life is?

80

One of the painful things I wonder about on page 229 is this: When you have had dreams, and they have come true, but then are shattered or taken away, how do you dream again?

Have you ever had this experience in life? If so, what was the dream that was taken away? Have you found a way to dream again?

82

Throughout the book I write about the power of "tears." For example, on pp. 229-230 I talk about the power of tears that helped sustain Pauline as she was dying, and their power to also sustain me in my grief.

Have you experienced this in your life? Are you able to let your tears fall for another, or do you try to keep them covered up?

I also write here about the power of God's tears, as did Pauline (185). Have you ever thought of God as crying with us in our suffering? Are there other ways you conceive of God's presence with us in our most difficult times?

One of the most difficult aspects of grieving is the revelation that we can't go on living in the past; that we need to find a way to begin to move into the future. On pp. 231-232 I struggle with this need to move on, addressing Pauline: "I must walk away from you. Not because I want to, but because I have to." (231) I go on: "How can I leave what was so precious to me? But I must in order to live again." (232)

What are your thoughts about and experiences with this aspect of life? How do we go about finding a way to move on beyond our grief? How do we help others move on beyond their losses?

86

Chapter 14: The Winter of My Spirituality: Rebirth, Yet Again (233)

This is a key chapter in my struggle to find a way to move on without Pauline. It is built around the experience of wanting so badly for the ones we love who have died to return to us. We want life back "the way it used to be." In fact, we might find ourselves feeling badly that we didn't "appreciate what we had at the time."

I begin by talking about "marriage vows" and the fact that even though we committed ourselves to loving until "death do us part" that we may find, after death, that we feel a need to continue honoring those vows. (234)

Can you relate to this? Has it happened to you? Can it be healthy to decide not to move on, and to live out the rest of your life staying committed to someone, even after they have died?

On p. 234 I grapple with the struggle between the "will and the heart." There are times in grief when we try to "will" ourselves toward healing and hope, but we find our feelings and heart drag behind.

Have you ever had this experience?

On pp. 238-239 I discuss the "fear of death," or lack thereof. Are you afraid to die? What are your thoughts about your own dying?

If you are afraid, can you think of any ways you might work with that fear?

I find profound the following statement I once heard: "I am not afraid of dying. I would just rather not be there when it happens."

How much of our fear of death is what we envision the actual experience to be, versus the more existential question of how death and life fit together?

On p. 239 I continue to struggle with "moving on." I begin to realize that for all the love and intimacy we may experience in life, that there is a way in which, at the beginning and at the end of life, each of us must make the journey alone. Pauline and I clung to each other as long as we could, but eventually she had to go on her own journey through death. And then I realized it would be unfair for me to get my greatest wish: that she would return to me. That would mean she would have to die again.

As I began to understand that, my thinking began to change. Just as Pauline had had to move on ahead without me, now I needed to find a way to move on without her: "Slowly I was beginning to realize and accept that Pauline had found her new life, and now I needed to find mine." (240)

What are your thoughts about this aspect of the spiritual journey we each must take? What feelings and emotions does it conjure up for you?

Chapter 15: Show Me the Way to Love (243)

In the spiritual life loneliness and solitude are at opposite poles. Loneliness is when you feel weak and alone, whether actually alone or in a crowd. Solitude is being at peace with yourself and the world, even while alone. At the end of Chapter 14 I sense a need to go deeper into the spiritual life (242) and on pp. 244-246 I describe the process through which I began to try to develop greater psychological and spiritual strength.

Are you comfortable being alone? Are you able to experience "solitude?"

How are solitude, prayer, music, reading and reflecting, worship and journaling able to give us greater insight and strength?

Throughout the book I talk about my growing and changing understanding of the relationship of God to suffering, pain and loss. I move from seeing everything that happens as being caused by God (God's Will theology) to coming to believe that much of life remains a **mystery**. What we can cling to is that God is always with us, crying with us. On p. 246 I wonder if this new theology can help me feel closer to God than I did after the deaths of my parents. And it did.

As you grew up, how did you understand the relationship of God to suffering? Do you believe the same now, or has your theology changed?

On p. 247 I write: "Once one understands that grief never ends, then it doesn't matter so much where one is in the grieving process. What does matter is that one begins to find a reason to live again, to love again."

What is your reaction to that statement?

Chapter 16: Easter: Lo, I Am with You Always (252)

On p. 253 I write: "No matter how you cut it, death is not a problem to be solved. It stares you in the face and refuses to move. It separates you from those you love and need and never gives them back."

Our tendency in life is to sugarcoat everything. One of the most difficult things I had to learn was that grief does not lead us back to where we once were. (254) It forever changes us, forcing us into a new life that we did not choose, and may have difficulty accepting.

What has been your experience with loss and grief? Where have you found some kind of resolution? What pain and suffering still lingers? What do you need most from others right now? What do others who are suffering need from you right now?

104

As difficult as it is to leave the past behind, and live into our new future, it is dangerous to refuse to move forward. As I write, "Wallowing in our pain endlessly turns the compassion and sympathy of others into pity and theologically is a refusal of grace." (255)

Have you experienced this last part in your own life or witnessed it in the lives of others? If so, what can break this cycle of despair?

I begin to find greater healing and hope as I move from grief over the past to gratitude for what I have experienced and what I continue to experience.

In what ways are you able to relate to my experience leaving the graves of my parents, after introducing them to Pauline:

> There was no great joy. No laugher. No overwhelming
> feeling of happiness. But there also was not a deep,
> cutting, agonizing pain. Just a quiet, irenic calm. Just
> a peaceful feeling of security, warm in the
> remembrance of how much I had been loved, secure
> in the knowledge that I was still loved, by family,
> by so many gracious friends, by God. (259)

108

What other thoughts or questions do you have when it comes to facing death and grief?

Are there any commitments you want to make now about how you will deal with death and grief in the future, both in your own life and in the lives of those dear to you?